The Good, the Bad & the Ugly

Judges

by Mark Baddeley

MATTHIAS MEDIA

The Good, the Bad and the Ugly
© Mark Baddeley, Matthias Media 2001

*For the general approach of these studies, and for many insights on
particular passages, the author would like to acknowledge his debt to
Barry Webb's book, "The book of Judges: an integrated reading"
(Sheffield: JSOT Press, 1987). Many thanks are due to Barry, not only
for his book, but for personal encouragement and comments in the
preparation of this manuscript.*

Published in the UK by
THE GOOD BOOK COMPANY
Elm House, 37 Elm Road
New Malden, Surrey KT3 3HB
Tel: 020-8942-0880
Fax: 020-8942-0990
e-mail: admin@thegoodbook.co.uk
Website: www.thegoodbook.co.uk

Scripture taken from the HOLY BIBLE, NEW INTERNATIONAL
VERSION. Copyright © 1973, 1978, 1984 International Bible
Society. Used by permission of Zondervan Publishers.

ISBN 1876326 29 8

Cover Illustration: Kirstie McAllister

Contents

How to make the most of these studies

1. What is an Interactive Bible Study?

These 'interactive' Bible studies are a bit like a guided tour of a famous city. The studies will take you through Judges, pointing out things along the way, filling in background details, and suggesting avenues for further exploration. But there is also time for you to do some sight-seeing of your own—to wander off, have a good look for yourself, and form your own conclusions.

In other words, we have designed these studies to fall half-way between a sermon and a set of unadorned Bible study questions. We want to provide stimulation and input and point you in the right direction, while leaving you to do a lot of the exploration and discovery yourself.

We hope that these studies will stimulate lots of 'interaction'—interaction with the Bible, with the things we've written, with your own current thoughts and attitudes, with other people as you discuss them, and with God as you talk to him about it all.

2. The format

Each study contains sections of text to introduce, summarize, suggest and provoke. We've left plenty of room in the margins for you to jot comments and questions as you read. Interspersed throughout the text are three types of 'interaction', each with their own symbol:

For starters

Questions to break the ice and get you thinking.

Investigate

Questions to help you investigate key parts of the Bible.

Think it Through

Questions to help you think through the implications of your discoveries and write down your own thoughts and reactions.

When you come to one of these symbols, you'll know that it's time to do some work of your own.

3. Suggestions for Individual Study

- Before you begin, pray that God would open your eyes to what he is saying in Judges and give you the spiritual strength to do something about it. You may be spurred to pray again at the end of the study.
- Work through the study, following the directions as you go. Write in the spaces provided.
- Resist the temptation to skip over the *Think it through* sections. It is important to think about the sections of text (rather than just accepting them as true) and to ponder the implications for your life. Writing these things down is a very valuable way to get your thoughts working.
- Take what opportunities you can to talk to others about what you've learnt.

4. Suggestions for Group Study

- Much of the above applies to group study as well. The studies are suitable for structured Bible study or cell groups, as well as for more informal pairs and threesomes. Get together with a friend/s and work through them at your own pace; use them as the basis for regular Bible study with your spouse. You don't need the formal structure of a 'group' to gain maximum benefit.

- It is *vital* that group members work through the study themselves *before* the group meets. The group discussion can take place comfortably in an hour (depending on how side-tracked you get!), but only if all the members have done the work and are familiar with the material.

- Spend most of the group time discussing the 'interactive' sections—*Investigate* and *Think it through*. Reading all the text together will take too long and should be unnecessary if the group members have done their preparation. You may wish to underline and read aloud particular paragraphs or sections of text that you think are important.

- The role of the group leader is to direct the course of the discussion and to try to draw the threads together at the end. This will mean a little extra preparation—underlining important sections of text to emphasize, working out which questions are worth concentrating on, and being sure of the main thrust of the study. Leaders will also probably want to work out approximately how long they'd like to spend on each part.

- We haven't included an 'answer guide' to the questions in the studies. This is a deliberate move. We want to give you a guided tour of Judges, not a lecture. There is more than enough in the text we have written and the questions we have asked to point you in what we think is the right direction. The rest is up to you.

Before you begin

We recommend that before you start on Study 1, you take the time to read right through Judges in one sitting. This will give you a feel for the direction and purpose of the whole book and help you greatly in looking at each passage in its context.

Starting well

Beth was in despair. Everything had started so well. Becoming a Christian in her late teens had been so exciting. She had joined a Bible Study Group and had enjoyed learning about Christ and the Bible. There she met Richard, a young Christian man. Friendship between them blossomed and grew into something more.

Then Richard began to pressure Beth to sleep with him. Confused, and scared to lose him, Beth agreed. "After all", she consoled herself, "we do love each other and we are both Christians."

Over time, guilt grew. Beth hated going to church, felt cold when she prayed, and stopped reading the Bible. She felt like a hypocrite, and God seemed unreal. Then Richard broke off the relationship.

For Beth, it felt as though she had lost everything. "Things weren't supposed to turn out like this", she thought. "Why did God let this happen?"

Stories such as this are disturbing. We prefer "happily-ever-after endings", where the challenges and threats are overcome and everything turns out well at the end. This is how we want life to be.

Israel's story in the Old Testament is the exact opposite. Things started with enormous potential. There were amazing promises given to Abraham that God would bless Israel and, through Israel, the world. Israel experienced a mighty redemption from slavery, with great signs and miracles under Moses. The initial entry into the Promised Land under Joshua went from strength to strength. By the time of Joshua's death, Israel was established in the Land. Yet, from this point on, things go sour. Israel's conquest stalls during the time of the judges and is only completed centuries later under David. Yet even David's victory is temporary—under David's descendants, Israel first suffers division into two separate kingdoms and then Exile from the Promised Land. All hopes have apparently been dashed and God's promises are unfulfilled.

Why did such a great story turn so bad? The book of Judges shows us why, and provides us with powerful warnings along the way.

Yet it does more than that. It also points ahead to the way in which God would fulfil his promises in the future.

So buckle down, as through these ten studies we relive some of Israel's most exciting times.

Investigate

Read Judges 1:1-20.

1. List all the successes Judah had in verses 1-20. What is your impression of how successful they have been?

Victorious in all Battles except vs 20

2. Why was this campaign necessary? (Gen 15:12-16; Deut 7:1-6; 9:4-5)

Vholy+chosen +Treasured possession.

① Gods Command
② To destroy the Canaanites Wickedness

3. How do Adoni-Bezek's words in 1:7 help us to understand what is happening?

Gods Punishment seen by Adoni-Bezek

4. What is your impression of Othniel and Acsah (1:12-15)? How do they contribute to the flow of the story?

5. What reason is given for Judah's success (1:19)? Why then do you think Judah couldn't succeed in the valleys?

(1) Chariots
(2) Broke Covenant - made treaties with Cannanites
(3) God was testing Israels faithfulness to obey his commands.
(4) An opportunity to develop army skills

Rwanda. Bosnia. Yugoslavia. East Timor. The words conjure pictures of violence and hatred, of genocide and ethnic cleansing. At first glance Israel's conquest of Canaan might seem similar—just another tribal conflict.

Yet, this campaign was radically different. It was a holy war, started and directed by God. Justice and redemption were its goals. The elimination of the Canaanites was both God's judgement on them and a necessary action to keep Israel from being corrupted by their evil. This military operation would be like a surgeon removing a cancerous growth. It would create a place where God's blessings promised in Genesis 12:1-3 could be enjoyed by Israel and, through Israel, the world.

Things start well; the picture is of total victory—with one exception. Although God is with them, Judah is unable to defeat the people of the plains with their iron chariots. It is unexplained, and the mystery is disturbing. But by it, we are prepared for the recounting of the other tribes' progress.

Investigate

Read Judges 1:21-36

1. What is your overall impression of Israel's success in these verses?

2. What do you think of the house of Joseph's actions in verses 22-26? Why?

3. Why do you think that some of the tribes used Canaanites for forced labour instead of driving them out?

4. What is the effect of leaving the Danites' situation until last? (vv. 34-36)

Another failure?

↓ Compromise with people they live with ÷ Not
doing what God had said.

Although Israel had started well with the account of Judah's conquests, the news turns increasingly sour as the different tribes are listed.

None of the other tribes enjoy successes approaching that of Judah. Two things are particularly disturbing.

First is the account of the conquest of the city of Luz in verses 23-26. This passage reminds us of the conquest of Jericho in Joshua 2-6. In both cases Israel makes a covenant with a Canaanite to preserve the life of the Canaanite. However, in the Jericho episode the initiative was with the Canaanite (Rahab) who threw her lot in with Israel and joined God's people. In Luz, it is the Israelites who initiate the covenant. The Canaanite, far from joining Israel, moves away a distance and rebuilds Luz. This preserves Canaanite idolatry in the middle of the Promised Land! The contrast between Luz and Jericho shows us that Israel's actions are no longer directed towards the elimination of Canaanite idolatry. Their goals are no longer God's goals.

The second disturbing note is struck in verses 27-34. The reports are increasingly bleak in these verses. First, we are told that the Canaanites continued to live among the Israelites. Then we are told that the Israelites lived among the Canaanites. Finally, we are told that the tribe of Dan is forced back into the hills out of their allotment of land. The initial good start has first slowed and then turned into a rout! Israel has not fulfilled the charge God gave her in the Law to clear the Promised Land of its inhabitants. The stage is set to hear God's word on this.

Investigate

Read Judges 2:1-5

1. What was Israel's obligation (2:2)?

-Gods Covenant not to mix with local Population

2. Compare God's commitment in verse 1 to God's action in verse 3. How would you reconcile these two statements?

Gods judgement came upon the Israelites because of their disobedience

3. Given what you have seen so far, how much of a difference do you think Israel's actions in verses 4-5 will make to the situation?

Not true repentence = only partial

4. In your own words, describe Israel's position by the end of 2:5.

The angel of the LORD[1] spells out the problem. God had promised never to break the covenant—he had committed himself to bless Israel. Yet the covenant *also* obligated Israel to keep God's commands. Israel had not done this. Israel's disobedience meant that she could no longer be a recipient of the promised blessings. God would not bless because Israel was not faithful to the covenant.

Israel's grief at the news did not remove the core problem. Obedience was necessary to receive the promised blessing. Yet Israel is proving to be incapable of the needed obedience. The final outcome of this is unclear, but what *is* clear is that it will create a change in Israel's environment. In 2:3 God declares that he would stop driving out the Canaanites from before Israel. Their presence would become a permanent feature, and they and their gods would continue to create trouble for Israel.

---

1. We will follow the normal English Bible convention of writing the revealed name of God—YHWH—as the LORD in small capitals.

Think it through

1. How does the fact that God was behind a holy war against the Canaanites make you feel? How does it fit with your understanding of what God is like?

2. What would you need to change to bring your understanding of God in line with the message of this passage? What does a holy war tell you about God's character and purposes?

3. Rather than obey God's command, Israel chose to make deals with the Canaanites to allow them to continue to live. Why do you think they acted this way?

4. *Read 1 Corinthians 10:1-14*

   a. In general, how does Israel's history serve as an example and lesson for us?

   b. Look back at your answer to question 3 (above). In what way are you tempted to act like Israel?

2

The heart of the problem

There are few things more disturbing to witness than the sight of people who have lost their memories. Familiar faces, preferred routines, even loved ones and the person's own name become unfamiliar.

We need to be able to remember in order to function as people. Our memories provide us with a sense of who we are; they orient us to life. Forgetting can render us helpless and disorientated, unable to act in our best interests.

Remembering was critical to Israel's life in the land, because her very existence was founded upon *knowing God and what he had done to save her.* It was this knowledge that enabled Israel to understand who she was. It enabled her to live the way she was supposed to. When Israel forgot God and forgot what God had done for her, she put her life in peril.

Investigate

Read Judges 2:6-13

1. How did Israel behave under Joshua and his elders?

2. Describe Israel's behaviour after Joshua and his elders were dead.

3. What made the difference? Why do you think this was so significant?

Read Judges 2:14-3:6

4. What was God's response to Israel's action (2:14-15)?

5. What effect did this have on Israel?

6. What did God do after this?

7. Why did God do this?

8. How did Israel respond to what God did (2:17, 19)?

9. How would you describe Israel in light of her behaviour?

10. What was God's final verdict on Israel? What did God do in light of Israel's actions?

11. What purpose did this serve and what was the result?

Judges 2:6-3:6 is a snapshot of the entire history of the Judges era. It begins with an event that occurred before those related in Chapter 1, and ends with the outcome of the era: Israel living in settled disobedience, intermarrying with Canaanites and worshipping their gods. The material in between 2:6 and 3:6 explains how this came to be.

Through it all, God remains in control. When Israel sins, the misfortune that follows is not accidental. It is the LORD God who hands them over to their enemies to be plundered and oppressed. And it is also God who is moved to pity, and who sends judges to deliver Israel from her bondage.

Yet, incredibly, Israel would not stop serving the gods, nor obey the LORD's commands. Despite God's mercy shown through the judges, Israel would not serve God the way Joshua's generation had. They did not listen to the judges when they were alive, and grew worse once they were dead. Although God alternated between judgement and pity, Israel stubbornly persisted in her practices.

And so God puts Israel to the test—he leaves the remaining nations in place. This serves three purposes. First, it is a judgement on Israel's refusal to obey God's Word (2:20). Second, it tests Israel's willingness to keep God's covenant (2:22, 3:4). Finally, it allows the generations after Joshua to learn holy war and so be involved in God's purposes (3:2).

Chapter 3:5-6 informs us of the outcome of the test. Israel completely failed. By the end of the Judges era she was living in the midst of the Canaanites, was intermarrying with them, and was serving their gods. In other words, Israel had abandoned God's project of conquest, and had rejected her unique relationship with God. Israel had proved that she was not prepared to walk in the LORD's way or to keep his covenant and commands.

The stories that follow fit into the period recounted in 2:6-3:6. They show Israel's repeated disobedience and how God continued to show justice and mercy to her. They demonstrate that the heart of Israel's problem was the problem of her heart.

Yet, these stories also suggest where the heart of the solution lies. It lies in God's mercy working through a deliverer that God raises up.

Think it through

1. Look up Ezekiel 36:25-28; Jeremiah 31:31-34 and Hebrews 8:6-12. What is God's ultimate solution to the problem of Israel's heart?

2. ***Read Hebrews 3:7-13.*** Why is it helpful to read and reflect upon Israel's hardness of heart?

3. What are some of the ways that our hearts can have the same problem as Israel? (Look up Jas 4:1-4 and 1 Jn 2:15-17 for some ideas.) What can you do about it?

4. "God is in control of good things but not bad." Would you agree with this? Why or why not?

5. How can God be loving and in control, yet bad things happen to his people (Jdg 2:20, 21 ; cf. Heb 12:4-11)?

3

Othniel and Ehud: The right stuff

The scene: a riot. A large crowd is trying to throw a man off the cliff near their village. They are beside themselves with anger. The man they are trying to kill is someone they know well; after all, he grew up among them.

What caused their anger? It may surprise you: the man had told them that God's salvation had arrived. He had told them what it would look like. And what he said was so disturbing, so scandalous, they tried to kill him.

Sound farfetched? This account can be found in Luke 4:16-29. It is the story of how the people of Jesus' home town tried to kill him when he proclaimed salvation to them. When God acts to save his people, it can be unsettling, even disturbing. This was true in Jesus' day. It was also true in the time of the judges[1], as we shall see. The account of the careers of the first three judges in Judges chapter 3 shows that it is a constant feature of God's saving work. God saves in scandalous ways.

---

1.   It is worth noting at this point that the Hebrew word translated 'judges' in most English Bibles means something a little different from what we would associate with a 'judge'. When we think of 'judges', we think of people who dispense justice in court, who hear cases and give verdicts. This was part of the function of the 'judge' in the ancient world, but it went further than that. A judge was a leader and a ruler; he not only heard cases and made decisions in disputes, he provided leadership for the community. As we shall see in the book of Judges, the 'judges' of that period were also military commanders-in-chief who were responsible for saving the people from their enemies.

Investigate

Read Judges 3:7-11

1. Fill out the following table:

Israel's action v. 7	
God's response v. 8	
Israel's action v. 9	
God's response v. 9	
What happens to the judge v. 10	
What the judge does v. 10	
The outcome v. 11	

2. Does Othniel seem to be a good choice as Judge to you? Why or why not (cf. Jdg 1:12-15)?

It is very satisfying when everything happens the way we think it should. We prefer things to occur in a way that seems logical and reasonable to us. This is what Othniel's career offers us.

Othniel is a very satisfying choice for judge. He is connected to Judah, the most successful conquering tribe in chapter 1. He is a holy-war hero and is related (by birth and marriage) to the great Caleb. He is the very image of a blue-blooded Israelite. He has all the credentials for the job. *Othniel is the model of what a judge should be. His career is the template that all later judges are to be compared to.*

And this comparison begins with Ehud and Shamgar…

Investigate

Read Judges 3:12-31

1. List everything in the account of Ehud that is similar to the account of Othniel (using the same kind of table as above).

Israel's action	
God's response	
Israel's action	
God's response	
What happens to the judge	
What the judge does	
The outcome	

2. What differences can you see?

3. Does Ehud seem to you to be as logical a choice for judge as Othniel? Why or why not?

4. What role did Ehud's handedness and Eglon's weight play in the assassination? How does this make you feel?

5. How do verses 22-26 contribute to the story? (What would be lost if these were missing?)

6. What was the outcome of Eglon's death?

7. What similarities do you see between Shamgar and Ehud?

James Bond. The name is synonymous with debonair antics and stylish charm. Ehud's story could almost be a plot for the Secret Service agent. He breezes into the enemy headquarters with a specially prepared hidden weapon, bluffs his way until he is alone with the master mind, eliminates him in a one-on-one confrontation, and then misdirects the henchmen so that they look like fools while he makes his escape.

The story is designed to impress us with Ehud's masterly dispatch of Eglon. It is clearly the most important thing for us to know about Ehud's career. Roughly three times as much space is spent on this (vv. 16-26) as on the battle that delivers Israel from Moab (vv. 27-30). The impression is that Eglon's death paves the way for the defeat of Moab.

Right at the start, we are informed of the three factors that will coalesce at the critical moment: Ehud's left-handedness, the special sword and Eglon's weight. Forewarned, we are able to savour the action when it occurs.

There is also a play on words in verses 19-20. The Hebrew word for 'message' is the same as the word for 'thing'. At the same time that Eglon is awaiting his "secret message from God", we the readers are anticipating the impact that the "secret thing from God" will make.

Finally, Eglon and his servants are implicitly ridiculed. There is emphasis on Eglon's fatness—"Eglon was a very fat man"—and his foolishness in sending away everyone at just the wrong moment. Similarly, his servants are portrayed as bumbling clowns. They wait with embarrassment at Eglon's long time in the toilet while Ehud escapes. This is black irony, for Eglon's bowels give way at the point of death (a detail omitted in the NIV). The scene is played for maximum effect, emphasizing that in comparison to Ehud, Eglon and his servants are powerless and ridiculous.

But there is also a troubling note to Ehud. For all the consummate skill he displays, he is nothing more than an assassin —unlike Othniel who led Israel to noble victory on the battlefield. The key to Ehud's victory is deception and the killing of a vulnerable man. Even worse is the fact that Ehud is left-handed. To be left-handed was considered a defect, a deformity—it was a stigma. (Even in English, the word 'sinister' also refers to the left hand). And yet this stigma is the key to the way Ehud delivers Israel. Finally, there is no indication that Israel was even aware of Ehud's plan and preparations. It is entirely possible that Ehud acted alone, without Israel's sanction.

Ehud is brilliant and we are encouraged to enjoy his dispatch of Eglon. Yet, he is also a troubling and scandalous figure—the lone left-handed assassin.

Shamgar is very like Ehud. Like Ehud, Shamgar delivers Israel by use of a non-standard weapon. His performance is also masterful—bludgeoning to death 600 Philistines. But he is also a troubling figure. Unlike the two previous judges we are not given Shamgar's tribal connections. The lack raises the possibility that he mightn't have any—that Israel's deliverer isn't even an Israelite!

Ehud and Shamgar show us the nature of God's deliverance. God's deliverance is both effortless and scandalous.

When God acts to save his people it does not always appear 'right' and 'understandable' as it did with Othniel. Sometimes God's saving work can seem (from a human point of view) to be offensive and incomprehensible, as it was with Ehud and Shamgar. This is especially true of God's greatest act of deliverance: Christ's death on the cross.

Think it through

1. Are there certain traits that must exist in someone before God can use him or her for his purposes?

2. What does it tell you about God that he is willing and able to deliver his people through the efforts of an Ehud or a Shamgar?

3. How should this change the way you perceive God? other people?

4. **Read 1 Corinthians 1:18-31.** What similarities can you see between this and the stories of Othniel, Ehud and Shamgar?

5. In what ways should this affect your understanding of the cross of Christ? How should it affect your proclamation of it?

6. In light of what you have looked at, what place should boasting have in your life? (cf. Jdg 3:10, 15, 28 ; 1 Cor 1:26-31)

Deborah and Barak: Some trust in chariots

For Starters

1. When do you find it hardest to believe God's Word?

Judges began by giving us the big picture view. It showed us what happened that led to the cycle of oppression and deliverance. It even showed us *why* it happened; that Israel would not keep to the covenant that the LORD made with her.

Then, with Barak, Ehud and Shamgar, God began to teach us about the nature of his salvation. He showed us that it is so surprising, so counter to our expectations, that it is shocking.

Now in chapters 4 and 5, we turn to an unusual pair who together do the work of one judge. Through their story, God has more to teach us about the unexpected nature of his deliverance. But these chapters have still more to say to us, including an example of what can happen when God's deliverer lacks faith in the God who delivers...

Investigate

Read Judges 4:1-10

1. Why do you think the narrator makes such a big deal about the iron chariots (cf 1:19)?

2. What is different about this judge (vv. 4-5)?

3. Summarize Deborah's message to Barak.

4. How does Barak respond?

5. How do you feel about this response? Why?

6. What is Deborah's response? At this point in the story, what do you think Deborah means by this?

Deborah's words in verse 9 make it clear that Barak has no right to lay down conditions. Obedience to God's command and trust in his promise is the response that God seeks.

Undoubtedly circumstances were unsettling for Barak. On the one hand, his enemy was armed with iron chariots, giving them an overwhelming tactical advantage against Israel's infantry. On the other hand, things within Israel weren't fitting in with the established pattern. This time the judge was a woman and a prophetess. Even more disturbingly, this time the judge was not the deliverer. Deborah had outsourced the tasking of delivering Israel to Barak. Judge and deliverance were separate.

Yet, by laying down a condition, Barak calls into question the certainty of God's promise. His condition implies that God's promise would be guaranteed *if the messenger was present.* God grants his request but he is informed that his lack of faith will mean that he will receive no honour from the forthcoming deliverance.

Investigate

Read Judges 4:10-24

1. Does the battle in verses 10-16 exactly follow Deborah's words in verses 6-7? What significance do you see in this?

2. How satisfied would you be with the story if it ended at verse 16? Why?

3. How would you have expected Jael to treat Sisera? Why?

4. How does she treat Sisera?

5. What does she do next (v. 21)?

6. Do you see any similarities between this episode and that of Ehud?

7. How does verse 22 fulfil Deborah's prophecy in verse 9? Is this a fitting judgement on Barak? Why or why not?

Barak need never have worried. The narrator leaves us in no doubt as to the certainty of God's Word. Everything Deborah said to Barak is fulfilled to the letter. First, the battle goes according to prophecy, and then Sisera is given into a woman's hand, depriving Barak of the honour of the deliverance.

Instead, the honour is given to Jael. This is a particularly surprising thing. Jael's people are neither part of Israel nor loyal to Israel. She is a Kenite, a descendant of Moses' father-in-law, and her husband had a treaty with Jabin. She is the wife of an ally of Israel's oppressor; it would be hard to imagine a less likely deliverer.

This reminds us of Ehud and Shamgar—that God's deliverance can be surprising and unexpected. In fact, this is just one of the many parallels between Ehud/Shamgar and Jael's slaying of Sisera. Like Ehud, Jael is a lone assassin. She slays her victim in a private place after tricking him into letting down his guard. Like Shamgar, Jael uses a makeshift weapon for the deed.

Yet, Jael takes the theme of God's surprising salvation one step further. With Ehud, we (the readers) knew what was going on from the beginning. We knew who the deliverer was and what weapon he would use. We could enjoy the *characters' ignorance* because *we had privileged knowledge.* But with Jael, we are just as ignorant as the characters; we find out what is happening only as the events occur. For the first time, we taste for ourselves the surprising nature of God's deliverance. Jael's action in verse 21 is almost as great a surprise to us as it was for Sisera. Nothing led us to expect God's Word being fulfilled in this way, but it is: Barak's glory in victory is given to a woman.

This episode concludes with a duet by Deborah and Barak that retells the story from a different perspective and adds several new notes.

Investigate

Read Judges 5:1-31

1. Some of the details of the song are a little difficult for us to follow, but how is God described in it?

2. How would you describe verses 24-31? What seems to be the main point of this section?

Two notes in this song warrant closer attention. For the first time since Othniel, Israel's deliverance is attributed explicitly to God. In verses 4-5, God is portrayed as the warrior going out to battle for his people. Then, when the battle is described in verses 19-23, it is in cosmic terms. There is no mention of Barak's force of 10,000; instead it is as though God fought with the forces of creation—the stars and the Kishon River. The song reminds us that God is the deliverer of his people, no matter the human agent he works through. *God* saves his people.

The other note is the retelling of Jael's deed in verses 24-31. The song clearly exalts in her slaying of Sisera. She is described as 'most blessed' among women and the details of her deception of Sisera, her slaying of Sisera, Sisera's dying moments, and the distress of Sisera's mother are all played up. This can appear almost sadistic to the 21st century reader. Yet verse 31 leaves us in no doubt that we are to rejoice in Jael's deed, for by it God has triumphed over his enemies, over those who oppress his people. Sisera's death is good because it is the defeat of God's enemy. Jael is blessed for she is an example to us of love for God by her wholehearted commitment to the welfare of God's people.

Some aspects of this whole episode we have seen before with Ehud and Shamgar—the strangeness of God's deliverance and the way in which God's people rejoice in his victory over his enemies.

But there are two striking new themes. First, God is free to discipline the person he has chosen to be the deliverer, in Barak's case by depriving him of honour. Just because someone has been chosen by God to accomplish a particular task does not give that person a special claim or hold on God. God's agents are not immune to God's discipline. We cannot attempt to manipulate God.

The other new theme is that God himself is the deliverer of his people. He is free to use any agent, whether human or not, or even none at all. But how ever he chooses to work, God alone is the source of salvation. This is an encouragement to us: God himself saves us; he does not leave it to someone else. It is also an ongoing challenge—we must never act in a way that attributes our salvation to anyone or anything other than God.

Think it through

1. How does the example of Jael challenge your view of:

   – God's attitude towards his enemies?

   – What it means to love God?

2. What difference should the fact that God himself has saved you make to the way you live?

3. In what ways can we be guilty of the same lack of faith in God's Word and the same attempts to try and manipulate him that Barak was?

4. ***Read Matthew 4:1-4.*** How does Jesus show us the way to avoid Barak's error?

5. Given what you have seen, how can Barak be held up as an example of faith in Hebrews 11:32? (Think: for all that Barak did wrong, what did he do that was right?)

Gideon: Whose kingdom?

Few things are more frustrating than a relationship in which the other person will not change no matter how often you challenge them. No matter what you do, they continue to act in ways that offend you.

By the time we reach chapter 6, the relationship between Yahweh and Israel has become like this. Prior to this account, Israel has done evil in the sight of the LORD on three separate occasions, and God has challenged Israel over it on three separate occasions. But as chapter 6 opens, Israel is yet again doing evil in God's sight and, as the account progresses, it is clear that the relationship is under strain.

Investigate

Read Judges 6:1-40

1. Describe Israel's situation under Midian's power.

2. What is God's response to Israel's cry (vv. 7-10)? Does he seem particularly keen to deliver? What is God's diagnosis of Israel's basic problem?

3. How does God describe Gideon? How does Gideon describe himself?

4. What is God's message to Gideon? What is Gideon's response?

5. What is God's first charge to Gideon (vv. 25-26)? What do you think of the way Gideon went about fulfilling it?

6. How do Gideon's neighbours respond to his actions (vv. 28-30)? What is the outcome?

7. Do you think Gideon's actions in verses 36-40 are good or bad? Why?

8. What is your impression of Gideon so far?

You could be excused for considering Gideon to be a world-class wimp by the end of chapter 6. When he is introduced to us, he is hiding from the Midianites in a wine press. He describes himself as the youngest member of the least family and carries out his first task by night out of fear of his neighbours. Finally, he asks for not one, but two signs that God would fulfil his Word. He hardly seems to be inspiring leadership material.

Yet the narrator subtly indicates that there is more to Gideon than meets the eye. No less than the angel of the LORD describes Gideon as a "mighty man" (or "valiant warrior"). The fact that Gideon could take ten of his servants suggests that he is not quite so powerless as he says. Finally, God's words in verse 14—literally, "Go in this your strength"—are ambiguous. Does God mean the strength Gideon has already or the strength that God will give him? There are hints that Gideon is actually a capable leader.

By joining these two strands together, our attention is taken away from Gideon's ability and directed to God as the true deliverer of Israel. Despite his personal resources, Gideon is diffident, almost backward about carrying out God's commission. He does not presumptuously push forward, confident in himself. He acts in faith on God's word in the end (Heb 11:32), but there is a lot of hesitation and requests for confirming signs along the way. Gideon's fearfulness shows us that the only hope he has is that God will fulfil his promise to deliver Israel through Gideon. We are left in no doubt that Gideon is not responsible for his successes.

Gideon's first mission is particularly important. The prophet's message of verses 8-10 focuses on Israel's idolatry as the major cause of God's discontent. By destroying Baal's altar and erecting an altar to Yahweh, Gideon was symbolically unseating Baal, the god of the Canaanites, and restoring Israel to the pure worship of the

LORD. A consequence of this symbolic action was that Baal was publicly shown to be powerless, unable even to contend for himself.

By the end of chapter 6, Israel has been mobilised, Baal has been dethroned and the Midianites have gathered for battle. All that is left is for the final battle to deliver Israel from Baal's minions.

Investigate

Read Judges 7:1-8:3

1. What reason does God give for reducing Gideon's numbers (v. 2)?

2. What is the size of Gideon's army before God starts reducing it? And after he has finished?

3. Given the size of Midian's forces, how would you be feeling when God began reducing your army? How does God relieve Gideon's fears?

4. After the events of the battle, what is your impression of Gideon?

Some of Gideon's potential comes to the fore in this section. The battle plan of verses 16-18 appears to have been his inspiration, as was the decision to send for Ephraim to cut off the Midianite retreat. Gideon also proves to be an adept diplomat, smoothing over the irate men of Ephraim.

Yet we are left in no doubt that *God* was responsible for the victory. On the one hand there is the incredible reduction of Gideon's army from an outnumbered 35,000 to a miniscule 300. Then there is the relatively long account of how Gideon's fears were eased on the night of the battle. Finally, the victory is explicitly attributed to Yahweh in verse 22.

Between Gideon's obedient faith and the explicitly clear actions of God, this is the least troublesome deliverance since Othniel. Everything seems to have gone right. Yet there is one more instalment to the Gideon saga…

Investigate

Read Judges 8:4-28

1. List all the times we are told that God acts in this chapter. What does this suggest to you?

2. What is Gideon's goal?

3. How does he respond to Succoth and Penuel when they refuse him aid? What do you think of this?

4. Describe the battle of verses 10-12. Who appears to be responsible for its success?

5. What was driving Gideon's pursuit? What do you think of this?

6. What reason does Israel give for its offer of rule to Gideon? Why do you think they have come to this conclusion? What is Gideon's response?

7. What is Gideon's request (vv. 24-25), and what is the outcome (vv. 26-27)?

8. Describe your view of Gideon now.

By the end of chapter 8 we can't help thinking, "How could this be the same Gideon we have watched from the start?"

Gideon now acts with greater confidence and competence. He drives his weary troops on in pursuit, demands support from cities he encounters, and single-handedly sets the Midian army to flight. He is not just a strong leader but also a ruthless one. His treatment of Succoth and Penuel is brutal, his slaying of Zebah and Zalmunna without remorse. It is only when his first-born son, Jether, is too afraid to kill that we are reminded that, not so long ago, Gideon was characterised by just this sort of fear. But now the strength that the angel of the LORD saw in Gideon (in 6:14) has reached its potential.

The change in Gideon is paralleled by a similar change in God's activity. In chapters 6 and 7, the LORD was actively involved— recruiting and commissioning Gideon, giving encouraging signs, directing the reduction of troop numbers and defeating the Midianite army. God takes a greater direct involvement in Gideon's life than with any other judge. Yet, in chapter 8 there is no mention by the narrator of any action by God. The implication is that God is not involved in these efforts, that they are not part of God's deliverance.

Thus, it comes as no surprise when Israel asks Gideon to rule them, on the basis that he has saved Israel. They seem to think that Gideon, and not the Lord, has been responsible for Israel's salvation. Gideon's actions have actually brought about the very thing that God was concerned to avoid in 7:2. Gideon's army was reduced to 300 to show that it was God alone who delivered Israel. After all, only God could defeat an innumerable army with a mere 300. Yet, Gideon has also defeated an immense force with that same 300. Gideon's actions in chapter 8 overturn God's concerns in chapter 7: he does what only God could do. Consequently, Israel has attributed her deliverance to someone other than God. And she has done this because of Gideon. Gideon is appropriately distressed by Israel's words but this cannot reverse what he has done. By his actions Gideon has led the people of God to attribute their salvation to someone other than God himself.

Why did Gideon act like this? We don't find out until verse 19. Gideon has been pursuing *a policy of personal revenge*—he is avenging the deaths of his brothers. God's program of deliverance for God's people has been co-opted by Gideon's personal agenda. Gideon has perverted God's salvation for his own ends.

Gideon warns us that we can have true faith and be involved in God's mission, and yet still be driven by our own agendas and act in ways that corrupt God's purposes.

Think it through

1. What did Gideon get right?

2. What was Gideon's basic problem? How did this show itself?

3. Consider your life: the people you know, the ways in which you contribute to the life of the Christians that you meet with. If Gideon's basic problem surfaced in your life, what would that look like? How would it display itself?

4. *Read Matthew 4:1-11.* How did Jesus demonstrate that his rule over God's people is not like Gideon's?

5. In light of what Jesus did, how can you take steps to safeguard against taking the path that Gideon took?

Abimelech: Nightmare on Shechem Street

Sometimes it can take a long time before the full impact of a person's life can be felt. Sometimes the greatest effects are only evident after their death. Gideon was like this. He accomplished much good while alive, but was also responsible for much harm to Israel's relationship with the LORD. However, the full consequences of his choices weren't felt until the generation after. That was when the nightmare *really* began.

Investigate

Read Judges 8:29-35

1. Describe Gideon's family situation.

2. Fill in the chart below:

PASSAGE	What Israel did
3:7	They did what was evil in the eyes of the Lord, worshipping the Baals and the Asherahs
3:12	
4:1	

PASSAGE	What Israel did
6:1	
8:33	

3. How did Israel treat the Lord? How did Israel treat Gideon's family? What link do you see?

What's in a name? Often the answer is 'nothing much'. But sometimes a person's name—especially a nickname—can tell you plenty. By the end of chapter 8, Gideon is an ambiguous character, both inspiring and worrying. Yet, he has a second name–Jerub-Baal–that tells you a lot about him.

He was given this name as a consequence of destroying Baal's altar back in chapter 6 (Jerub-Baal means 'he contends against Baal'). Gideon's other name reminds us that, for all his failures, he is not merely a private individual. He is the LORD's champion and chosen deliverer. He symbolises the worship of the LORD as opposed to Baal. He is a standing challenge to Baal.

By using 'Jerub-Baal' rather than 'Gideon' the narrator is helping us to see that Israel's treatment of Jerub-Baal's family is connected to their treatment of the LORD. The story that follows is about more than just politics; it is about the rejection of the LORD symbolised by the treatment of the family of Jerub-Baal. A similar point is made by verse 33: rather than the normal 'Israel did evil in the eyes of the LORD', the narrator focuses on the fact that Israel made 'Baal of the covenant' their god (Baal-Berith means 'Baal of the covenant'). Behind this story is the issue of Israel rejecting their covenant with the LORD in favour of Baal.

Yet the story does have a political theme as well. Gideon's story finished on a sour note as Israel offered to make Gideon king. Gideon rejected the offer, but as this scene opens we find that the issue of kingship is still lurking. Gideon had seventy sons by "many wives". This was typical royal dynastic behaviour for the period, and was explicitly forbidden by God (see Deut 17:17). Even worse, one of Gideon's sons is named 'Abimelech' which means 'my father is king'. For all his words to the contrary, the suggestion is that Gideon has acted like a *de facto* king.

Investigate

Read Judges 9:1-21

1. What is Abimelech's proposition (vv. 1-2)? Why is it accepted?

2. From where does Shechem acquire the money for Abimelech? What does Abimelech do with it?

3. Jothan proclaims his fable from Mt Gerizim. What significance do you think this has (cf. Deut 27:11-26)?

4. What seems to be the point of Jotham's fable (vv. 7-15)?

5. How does he apply it?

The importance of names continues. Shechem is the support base for Abimelech's grasp for power. It is a place with great significance for Israel. It had figured in the careers of the patriarchs Abraham, Jacob and Joseph. It had an important role in Israel's life—it was a town set aside for the Levites, and was a town of refuge, a place where someone who accidentally killed another could find refuge (see Jos 21:21). Most importantly of all, it was at Shechem that Joshua renewed Israel's covenant relationship with the LORD (Jos 24:25). Shechem was a name that had connotations for Israel's covenant with God.

Thus, the scene that unfolds has a nightmare-like quality. Everything has been distorted. Far from being a refuge from unjust killing, Shechem strengthens Abimelech to kill all of his brothers, Jerub-Baal's sons. Instead of being a centre of the covenant of the LORD, Shechem uses money from the temple of 'Baal of the covenant' to support Abimelech. And Jotham (of the tribe of Joseph) stands on Mt Gerizim to pronounce not a blessing, but an implicit curse on the murderous covenant-breakers. The place of blessing has become a place of curse. Everything Shechem stands for has been perverted.

For his part, Abimelech has become Jerub-Baal's opposite. His pitch to the lords of Shechem succeeds because he distances himself from his father and emphasises his kinship with Shechem. Unlike Gideon, who refused kingship because the LORD was

Israel's deliverer, Abimelech seeks to be king on the basis of tribal connections. Also unlike Gideon, who mobilised his army as a consequence of the Spirit's annointing (6:34-35), Abimelech hires a mercenary force with Baal's money. It appears as though the challenge 'let Baal contend' has finally been taken up. Someone who is prepared to fight for Baal has arisen–from Jerub-Baal's own family. Abimelech has become king through kinship and the patronage of Baal.

In light of these events, Jotham's speech is a condemnation and not a warning. His fable makes it clear what he thinks of the deal between Shechem and Abimelech. Olive trees, fig trees and vines were all profitable agriculture, while brambles were noxious pests. The implication is that Abimelech is a 'worthless fellow', only capable of destruction not rewards.

Accordingly, Jotham's words in verses 16-19 are savagely ironic. There can be no doubt that Shechem has not dealt in good faith and honour. Jotham has made use of normal language from Israel's covenant with the LORD to make his point. Shechem has acted in such a way toward Jerub-Baal's family that they can only expect a curse and not blessing in return.

Investigate

Read Judges 9:22-57

1. What is Jotham's curse in v20? What happens in verses 46-49?

2. How does Abimelech die? What is fitting about this? (cf. vv. 5, 18, 46-49)

3. What is God's purpose in all these events (vv. 23-24, 56-57)?

Jotham spoke more truly than he could have known. Fire from Abimelech does consume Shechem. Shechem experiences a full turning of the circle. In the beginning, they used Baal's money to enable Abimelech to hire a mercenary force. That same mercenary army kills them while they take refuge in the temple that they got the money from. ("El" was the general word for god; the narrator is emphasising that their god was Baal, cf. 9:27.) They are killed by the very forces that were hired with Baal's money. Their evil has been turned back on their own heads.

This poetic justice operates right through this final section. *Everybody's* evil is turned back on them; they suffer the same evil that they have done. Shechem ambushes and is ambushed (9:25 cf. 9:34); Abimelech's appeal to Shechem is paralleled by Gaal's appeal (9:2 cf. 9:28). Abimelech's fate is particularly poetic. The fact that he killed his brothers *on one stone* has been mentioned twice (9:5, 18). He himself is killed *by one stone*—a thrown upper millstone (9:53). The punishment fits the crime.

None of this is accidental. Both at the start of this section (9:23-24) and at the conclusion (9:56-57), we are told why all these things happened. *God* is behind these events. He sends an evil spirit in judgement on both Abimelech and Shechem. Unlike the Spirit of the LORD that empowers his judges, this evil spirit is sent to judge a king. God is in control of the evil of Abimelech and Shechem, and works through it to judge them both.

The result of God's judgement is good for Israel. Upon Abimelech's death, they go home. It is almost as though they woke up from the nightmare. God's judgement has acted like surgery, removing the cancer of evil from Israel.

God's actions could have been much worse for Israel. Behind the events of this chapter is the issue of Israel's covenant. Shechem's treatment of Jerub-Baal's family was merely a symptom of a far deeper problem. Israel had rejected their covenant with the LORD and had chosen a covenant with Baal. Gaal's speech in verses 28-29 demonstrates that far more was at stake than the affairs of a family and a local town. Gaal's words refer back to a grim incident in Genesis 34. At that time, Hamor, the king of Shechem, sought to have the fledgling Israelite nation intermarry with the Canaanites living in Shechem and become one people with them. Now again the same choice faced Israel at Shechem, but this time they caved in to the temptation. They desired to become like the nations in their midst, to reject the LORD and enter into relationship with Baal. Baal was their god. The events of the chapter remind us how stupid such a choice was. Baal is inactive and powerless throughout the chapter, and proves in the end to be a source of destruction to those that sought refuge in him.

Think it through

1. Summarise what you have learned about God from this passage.

2. How should you live in light of this?

3. "Do not be deceived: God cannot be mocked. A man reaps what he sows." (Gal 6:7). This has been graphically illustrated by Abimelech. In what ways do you see the same principle at work:

   – in people you know?

   – in your own life?

4. How certain is God's judgement on his enemies (see 2 Thess 1:5-12)? How should this affect our response to evil?

Jephthah: Doing the repentance thing

The last two studies have begun to peel back the problems with Israel's heart. Gideon demonstrated the problems of corrupt service. He attempted to pursue his own agendas as well as God's, and led Israel back into idolatry. Israel went even further under his son Abimelech. Abimelech's treatment of Gideon's family reflected Israel's treatment of the LORD. Despite God's saving work, Israel entered into a covenant relationship with Baal. God brought Abimelech's reign to an end, but we are left wondering: Does Israel understand what it means to be in relationship with the LORD?

Investigate

Read Judges 10:1-11:28

1. What is Israel's situation in the opening nine verses of chapter 10? How does this compare with previous episodes?

2. What is God's response to their cry? What is God's attitude towards them (in verses 11-16)?

3. What is your impression of Jephthah when you first meet him? Who does he remind you of?

4. How is the elders' treatment of Jephthah similar to Israel's treatment of God?

5. What is the main point of Jephthah's message to the King of Ammon (in 11:12-28)?

For the first time, we are given the details of Israel's cry to the LORD (10:10). On the face of it, their appeal seems genuine—they confess their sin (10:10, 15), they place themselves in God's hands (10:15), and they stop their idolatry (10:16). Yet the LORD's words in 10:11-14 indicate that he has seen all of this before, many times before. Israel always does what is needed to enlist God's help when in distress. She 'repents'. But as soon as the emergency is over, Israel goes back to her gods. The LORD's conclusion in 10:14 indicates just how fed up he is with Israel's behaviour: he implicitly refuses to intervene. Yet the LORD is clearly torn—verse 16 declares that he can no longer bear to see Israel suffer. What will God do when he is pulled in opposite directions?

Israel's helplessness is demonstrated in the events that follow. In the wake of the Ammonite invasion, Israel mingles around, speaking to one another, looking for someone to lead Israel. It is clear that the 'gods' are powerless to save. Turned away by the LORD, Israel must look for a leader to save them.

Enter Jephthah. He creates mixed feelings. Our sympathy is

aroused by his unfair treatment by his brothers. Yet there is also alarm: he is very similar to Abimelech. Abimelech, remember, was the son of a concubine, had conflict with his father's legitimate sons, and formed an army made up of worthless men. Jephthah is the son of a prostitute, has conflict with his father's legitimate sons, and forms an army made up of outlaws/adventurers. Given Abimelech's record, what is Jephthah capable of?

However, Jephthah quickly wins our respect. The elders think that they can obtain Jephthah's services easily enough, but he proves to be more than a match for them. In fact, his words to them are very like God's words to Israel in chapter 10. He is like a living illustration of the problem between Israel and God: they go running to the one they have rejected when they are in trouble, and promise to let him be their true king once he has triumphed. However, as we shall see, Jephthah not only represents God's deliverance of Israel on this occasion, he is also a mini-version of Israel herself. But more of that in due course.

Jephthah is installed as head (11:11). He then sets about dealing with the real problem: the king of Ammon. It is clear that this issue will not be resolved peaceably: Israel is in no position to surrender all the land that is demanded (11:13). Again, Jephthah wins our respect with his competence with words. He takes the part of the Israelite statesman, speaking with regal authority, "You have come to fight *me*, against *my* land" (11:12, the NIV wrongly renders this as plural). He recounts a masterful summary of Israel's history to show that Ammon's actions are wrong, and concludes by publicly placing the whole matter into the hands of the LORD.

Two questions are left hanging as we read these events. First, what are we to make of Jephthah? He regularly brings the LORD into his speech—attributing victory to him (11:9), speaking all his words before the LORD (11:11) and publicly calling on the LORD to act with justice and uphold Israel's case (11:27). Yet, we know that he has a vested interest in the outcome of the upcoming battle—he will only be confirmed as head over Gilead if he has victory. Are Jephthah's words expressions of his commitment to God and God's people, or are they a clever attempt to force God's hand? Or a bit of both?

Second, what does the LORD think of Jephthah? In previous episodes the LORD clearly chooses a deliverer. There is no indication that Jephthah is anything other than a human choice. What is God's view of Jephthah?

With these questions in our minds, we read on.

Investigate

Read Judges 11:29-12:15

1. How do we know God is now with Jephthah?

2. What is your view of Jephthah's vow? Why do you think he made it?

3. What is the outcome of Jephthah's vow?

4. Who has your sympathies: Jephthah or the daughter of Jephthah? Why?

5. What are your feelings about Jephthah's actions in 12:1-7? How do his actions compare with Gideon's dealing with the Ephraimites in chapter 8:1-3?

6. What does the whole story of Jephthah tell us about Israel's relationship with God at that time?

Deliverance comes at a terrible price. It costs Jephthah and his household personally, and Israel publicly.

The battle in 12:1-7 is tragic. Rather than peace, deliverance leads first to harsh words and then to brother killing brother in a terrible slaughter. There have already been indications in Judges that the unity of God's people is coming apart as they turn away from God. Deborah and Barak's song mentions tribes that did not come to the battle (5:15-17). Further, Gideon, like Jephthah, also had a conflict with Ephraim (8:1-3). Gideon only narrowly avoided a war by clever diplomacy.

Yet, unlike Gideon, Jephthah does not even try diplomacy—despite the fact that he is very good with words. He accuses Ephraim of not coming when called, and rather than seeking peace and the welfare of Israel, he appears to be concerned only for his interests as the leader of Gilead. He identifies himself with Gilead not Israel—'I and my people' (12:2)—and the outcome of the battle is that he increases his rule to all Israel (12:7). Most troubling of all, by taking the fords, Gilead treats their brother Israelites in the same way that Israel had treated her oppressors in previous episodes (3:27-30, 7:24-28). Jephthah's pursuit of his own goals has led to a tragic and destructive disunity among the people of God.

Even Jephthah's family picks up the tragic tab for his ambition. His vow leads to the death of his only daughter. The account stresses her virginity (11:37, 38, 39) and the fact that she is an only daughter (11:34)—the vow leaves both Jephthah and his daughter childless. Jephthah's distress at the death of his daughter is clear (11:35), yet it seems to be focused purely on himself. Despite the fact that she is the one doomed, he has no words of comfort for her.

In contrast to Jephthah's somewhat self-centred words, his daughter is full of innocent delight at his return (11:34), and full of courageous submission to her fate. She neither reproaches her father nor complains against her lot (11:36-37).

At one level, Jephthah's vow can be understood. Though he has publicly committed the justice of the matter to the LORD (11:27) his own experience may well suggest that he can't expect justice (11:2, 7). He seeks to cut a deal with the LORD, a contract whereby he can be assured of God's aid. The irony of course, is that *we* know his vow is unnecessary—11:29 has told us that God has empowered him as Israel's deliverer. He is trying to buy help already given freely.

Jephthah's vow mirrors the first two dialogues of this episode. Like Israel, Jephthah tries to guarantee God's deliverance by treating the covenant as though it is a mere contract. Israel thought that the LORD would be bound to deliver them if they *did the repentance thing*. Jephthah similarly tries to force God's help. Like the elders, Jephthah tries to buy the help for the lowest price possible. Like Israel, Jephthah tries to manipulate the LORD.

This is the tragedy of Jephthah. His words in 11:35 are literally: "I have opened my mouth to the LORD"; and Jephthah's name means literally 'he opens'. He is *good* at opening his mouth. His error was to think that he could relate to the LORD in the same way as he did with everyone else. The LORD uses Jephthah to deliver Israel but never gives approval, leaving Jephthah and Israel to the consequences of their manipulations.

There is more to relating to God than taking God's name on one's tongue. The relationship that God offers is not a clever contract that can be manipulated to advance selfish ambitions.

Thinking it through

1. Do you think there is any link between Israel's internal disunity and conflict, and their worshipping of other gods?

2. What false gods are modern Christians tempted to follow? And how does this bring conflict into relationships?

3. Israel presumed on God's forgiveness. They thought that when things got bad they could 'do the repentance thing' and God would deliver them. How are we tempted to do the same as Christians?

4. How does this whole episode add to your understanding of God? What implications should this have for the way you live?

5. What does Jephthah's story reveal about the wrong way to use the tongue in God's service?

6. What does Romans 10:9-13 and James 3:1-12 have to say about the right way to use the tongue?

Samson: We don't need another hero

In Judges 13-16 we come to perhaps the most famous character in the book: Samson, the strong man with a soft heart for the wrong sort of woman. Yet, as we shall see, Samson's story is not just a ripping yarn with a high body count. It is the last of the stories in the book about a saving judge bringing deliverance to wayward Israel. And in these chapters, both Israel and the judge himself seem to have sunk to new depths.

Investigate

Read Judges 13:1-25

1. In Judges 1-12, we have seen a standard pattern of sin, judgement and deliverance (e.g. Jdg 4:1-4). Can you spot what's different this time?

2. What is the angel's message to Manoah's wife? (13:3-5)

3. **Read Numbers 6:1-8.** What did it mean to be a Nazirite? What similarities and differences do you see between this account and the angel's words to Manoah's wife?

4. Who is the more likeable character in the story: Manoah or his wife? Why?

The first surprise in this chapter is the glaring absence of any call to the LORD by Israel. It appears that Israel has come to terms with her bondage and does not desire deliverance. With Jephthah, God delivered Israel *despite* her 'repentance'. This time God will deliver *without* any cry to him. As the following story will show, *God alone desires the overthrow of the Philistines and the deliverance of Israel.*

Manoah and his wife are striking opposites. Manoah cannot recognise that the messenger is the angel of the LORD (13:16), but once he does, he wrongly thinks that he will die because of it (13:22). He is not content with the word that God delivered and seeks to have it again (13:8, 12), and even to have it extended (13:17-18). Manoah represents all the problems that we have seen in Israel's response to God.

In contrast, his wife is a model of faith and submission. She recognises the messenger when she sees him (13:6), accepts God's word without asking for more (13:6) and draws the right implication from his appearance (13:23). The angel appears twice, both times to her, and both times when she is alone and not with Manoah. In her faith and her submission to God's word, she finds God's approval.

It is a surprising word that God brings to Manoah's wife. This is the first time that the commissioning of God's judge has happened before his birth! This judge has been dedicated to God's saving purposes even before he is born. In fact, his whole reason for being born is to deliver Israel. We can only wonder: what great things are in store for him?

Samson's birth is amazing. Yet, within God's plan it only hinted at something greater.

Investigate

Read Luke 1:26-38

1. What similarities and differences do you see between the birth of Jesus and that of Samson?

2. What similarities do you see between Mary and Manoah's wife?

Now read Judges 14:1-15:20

3. What do you think of Samson's desire for a Philistine wife (14:1-4)? What was God's role in this?

4. How do the Philistine's get the secret to Samson's riddle (14:15-18)? What is the result (14:19-20)?

5. How justifiable do you think Samson's actions are in 15:3-5 and 15:7-8? What is the result on each occasion?

6. What is Judah's role in these events (15:9-13)? What is the result (15:14-17)?

The gulf between the LORD's agenda and everyone else's continues. Samson's parents don't seem particularly concerned about Philistine oppression. Judah, the great conquering tribe of chapter 1, are now a shadow of their former selves. They rebuke Samson with the question, "Don't you know that the Philistines are rulers over us?" They are even prepared to hand their deliverer over to their oppressors. Worst of all is Samson himself. *Killing* Philistines seems to be the last thing on his mind. He seems more interested in marrying them.

However, the narrator makes it clear that God is at work through all of this. Samson's desire for a Philistine wife is, we are told, "from the LORD" (14:4). As events unfold, we can begin to see God's purpose fulfilled. First thirty Philistines are slain, then their harvest is destroyed, then many are slaughtered, and it culminates in the death of one thousand soldiers. Samson's actions in all this are questionable—his words indicate that his moral ground is just as low as that of the Philistines (15:11 cf. 15:10). Nonetheless, in it all we are able to see the fulfilling of the angel's promise: "he will begin the deliverance of Israel from the hands of the Philistines" (13:5).

Investigate

Read Judges 16:1-31

1. The events of 16:1-3 follow a familiar pattern. Can you see what it is?

2. How is this pattern repeated in the rest of the chapter?

3. What is motivating Samson (16:4)? Delilah (16:5)?

4. How is Samson portrayed in 16:6-17. What do you think of him?

5. How do the Philistines interpret their capture of Samson (16:23-24)? What is ironic about this (cf. 16:20, 22)?

6. What is the final result of all these events?

In case we missed the pattern of Samson's life, 16:1-3 runs us through it again in microcosm. Samson is attracted to a Philistine woman, this leaves him vulnerable, the Philistines think they have him in their power, but they are left weaker than before (as their fortress city is rendered gateless).

Third time around, however, and the story takes on a new poignancy. Solomon has not merely found a woman that he likes the look of or who is available for money. He *loves* Delilah. The tragedy is that, though Delilah accuses Samson of not loving her, she does not love him. He is merely a source of money. Samson's love is not returned. Even worse, his love for Delilah leads to his subjection.

Samson's teasing answers to Delilah circle in to the real issue: the cutting of his hair. In one sense, it is surprising that the LORD leaves Samson when the hair is cut. Samson hasn't kept *any* of the Nazirite rules—why should the hair be important? Yet, the cutting of Samson's hair seems to be of great significance. No less than three times in verses 17-18 we are told that this issue is "everything" or "all that was in his heart". Samson's long hair was the symbol of his special relationship with the LORD. It was the sign that he was not like "any other man" but that God had chosen him for a special role that entailed special restrictions on his behaviour. His continual pursuit of Philistine women suggests that he never accepted his role as deliverer—he *wanted* to be like any other man.

At this point, Samson reminds us of Israel. Just like Samson, Israel had been chosen before she even existed. She had a special relationship with the LORD that had its own symbols and responsibilities. Just like Samson, Israel never embraced her calling—she continually chased after foreign gods. And, just like Samson, Israel's love for the idols led to her enslavement. Samson only seems to be reconciled to his part in God's purposes at the point of death. Only when he is blind does he begin to see things

God's way. Samson's fate raises the question: just how low will God have to bring Israel before they too are reconciled to their place in God's plan? Samson shows us the tragic consequences of not living life in step with our relationship with God.

Yet Samson's picture is not all black. He also illustrates the nature of true faith. Israel thought they could guarantee God's response by going through the right motions. Samson calls on the LORD twice (15:18; 16:28). On both occasions, he places his life in God's hands. He confesses that his life and death lie in God's power, and he entrusts himself to God. Faith is not presumption, but confident trust in God.

Finally, Samson is a pattern of deliverance. In the midst of judgement, defeat and death, with the enemies of God congratulating themselves, God nevertheless wins a great victory. The man of God—alone, forsaken, being mocked by the crowd—stretches out his arms, defeats the enemy and delivers his people through his own death. The parallels with the salvation won by the Lord Jesus are clear enough. Indeed, Matthew quotes the words of the angel regarding Samson as being a prophecy about Jesus (Matt 2:23).

The differences between Samson and Jesus are just as plain. Samson is a reluctant and sinful deliverer, whose failings mirror those of Israel herself. Jesus was a faithful and obedient deliverer, who embodied all that Israel was meant to be.

Think it through

1. Is it possible to live well while rejecting God? Why or why not?

2. How would the desire to 'be as any other man' look in your life?

3. What have you learned about the nature of faith from Samson?

4. In what ways does the story of Samson add to your understanding of God and how he works?

5. Read Acts 2:22-24; 4:27-28; 1 Corinthians 2:6-8. How does the death of the Lord Jesus Christ demonstrate God's power over human evil?

Give me that old time religion

"Israel again did evil in the eyes of the lord."

This phrase has been tolling like a bell throughout the book of Judges. Israel knew that idolatry was wrong, that it offended God, and that it was a flagrant breach of his covenant with them. They had seen the judgement and oppression that it led to, time and time again. And yet, like a dog returning to its vomit, they just couldn't keep away from it. What did they think it would achieve? What was the underlying attitude that made idolatry so attractive to them?

Chapters 17 and 18 give us an insight into this, and a timely warning for us.

Investigate

Read Judges 17:1-13

1. Write a sentence or two giving your impression of the following characters. What do you think of each?

   • Micah

   • Micah's mother

• the Levite

2. What problems do you see with Micah's religion?

3. What does Micah think the effect of his efforts will be?

4. Does the author of Judges make any comment on the situation in this chapter?

Chapter 17 is almost a farce. Micah's name means "Who is like the LORD?". But it seems as though no-one understands what this means, least of all Micah. He is a thief, and a self-made man when it comes to religion—he has created his own shrine, ephod and priesthood.

At the beginning of chapter 17 he is under a curse arising from his theft of his mother's money. By the end of the chapter, he believes that he has guaranteed God's favour. We are not convinced. The stolen money is dedicated to the LORD to make into an idol—an appalling contradiction that seems to bother no-one.

The passage is full of these sorts of disturbing contradictions. First, Micah appoints one of his sons to be his priest, passing the idolatry to the next generation, as his mother had passed it to him.

Then a Levite turns up who seems to have no place to go. Why is this? Has Israel ceased to look after the Levites and provide cities for them as the Law required? Then the Levite readily agrees to become Micah's own personal priest.

The narrator's dry comment of verse 6 seems to sum up the situation. Israel is spiralling into lawlessness. Everyone is doing what is right in their own eyes, with scant regard for God. Nevertheless, Micah still thinks that he has God figured out. Despite the catalogue of lawlessness and disobedience, Micah is sure that he is in God's good books because he has fulfilled one minor ritual aspect of the Law—the priest in his idolatrous little home-made shrine is a *Levite*, the right kind of priest!

We are left wondering at the end of chapter 17: Will Micah indeed prosper, as he believes? Will the Levite bring blessing on him?

Investigate

Read Judges 18:1-31

1. Why are the Danites on the move? (cf. Jdg 1:34)

2. What makes the spies turn aside to Micah's house? What is ironic about this?

3. What do you think motivates the Levite (18:4)?

4. What do you think of the Danites' actions in 18:14-21? What about the actions of the Levite in 18:18-20?

5. What is Micah's problem?

6. How impressed are you with Dan's conquest? Why?

7. What hint is there that the Levite will not be a blessing to the Danites either?

No doubt the Danites thought that, like Micah, they were *guaranteed* God's blessing. They had the ephod and idols of Micah's religion, and their priest was a descendant of Moses! Yet the narrator leaves us in no doubt that this couldn't be further from the truth.

The Levite was actually the *cause* of Micah's downfall. The spies only turned aside because they heard his voice and recognised it. His words in 18:4 and his actions in 18:19-20 demonstrate that he is mercenary to the core. He betrays Micah as soon as a better deal was offered. His only motivation is his own gain. For this Levite, religion is a source of wealth and honour. His ministry is no guarantee of blessing.

The ephod and idols are shown to be worse than useless as well. When he chases the Danites, Micah is challenged, "What's the matter with you?" In his distress, his words reveal him: "What else do I have?" Without his man-made religion, he is nothing. He believed that his idolatry would guarantee God's favour. In fact, it rendered him as vulnerable and powerless as the idols themselves.

The Danites appear, on the surface, to have God's blessing. Their spies receive an oracle that God is with them. They encourage their tribesmen that God has given land to them. The conquest meets with success—the first time since chapter 1 that we have heard mention of Israel continuing the mandate of conquest.

But scratch the surface, and things aren't so good. The Danites, like Micah, steal from fellow-Israelites. It is hard to take seriously the made to order oracle from the mercenary priest. While the spies talk piously, their confidence seems to be at least as much in the vulnerability of the land's inhabitants; a fact that is stressed three times (18:7, 10, 27-28). This is no heroic conquest. It is no example of faith.

This is reinforced by the sending of the spies. The spies remind us of Moses and the successful conquest under Joshua (Nu 13; Josh 2). This parallel with the earlier accounts increases the contrast. Israel possessed their inheritance under Joshua; Dan's actions are due to their failure to possess their inheritance (18:1 cf 1:34). Dan's 'conquest' is actually a retreat!

Going by the comment in 18:30, it seems that the Danites' religious site operated for centuries—possibly until the Assyrian Exile. No doubt its pedigree (with Moses in the family tree) and its antiquity encouraged people to trust it. Indeed, like Micah, they may have thought that its existence gave them a hold on God. They may have thought that it guaranteed God's favour. But just as Micah discovered on a personal level that this wasn't true, so the Danites and Israel discovered on a national level that the idols and false religion led to only one thing—God's judgement, and the captivity of the land.

The words of 17:6 describe this whole passage. For Israel, everyone did as they saw fit—idolatry was good in their eyes.

Think it through

1. What have you learnt from these chapters about what God is like?

2. What have you learnt about the underlying reasons for Israel's constant idolatry?

3. How do you think Christians can be tempted to think that they are guaranteed God's blessing by some external ritual or form?

4. How are Christians, in fact, guaranteed God's blessing?

5. Are Christians completely immune from falling into idolatry and faithlessness? (Look up Ephesians 5:5-6.)

6. In what areas are you in danger?

Full circle

Over the last nine studies, we have been on a whirlwind tour of Israel's life during the time of the judges. Along the way the book has had plenty to say about the character of God's salvation, about some of the ways people sin, and why it was that Israel never got a firm hold on the promises of God. Let's do a quick recap.

In the first two studies we were given the background information we needed to understand the accounts of the different judges. We saw that Israel didn't complete Joshua's conquest of the Promised Land, but allowed the Canaanites to live. Chapter 2 revealed that this military failure was the result of a far greater failure, a failure to remember the LORD and his saving work. Because of this double failure, Israel repeatedly followed false gods and was subjected to the peoples of those gods. This was God's judgement upon Israel.

However, God was also merciful to them, and this took a particular form. Time and time again God raised up a judge to rescue Israel from their bondage. These deliverers were often not the choice we would expect, and often saved Israel in scandalous ways, as we saw with Ehud and Jael. Still others were very flawed heroes: Barak placed conditions on his obedience, Gideon pursued his own agendas, and Jephthah tried to cut a deal with God. There was even one man, Gideon's son Abimelech, who was the opposite of everything the judges stood for, an anti-judge.

Through it all, God never let us forget what the basic problem was. As each new episode began we heard the refrain, "Israel again did evil in the eyes of the LORD". This evil was the evil of idolatry, following gods and not the LORD, and it was this evil that resulted in Israel's bondage time and time and time again.

The final judge was Samson, the most contradictory one of the group. Set apart from before his birth for God's saving purposes, he spent his life chasing the women of the people he should have been delivering Israel from. He symbolised everything that was wrong with Israel: just as he followed foreign women and fought against his special role, so Israel followed foreign gods and fought against their special role.

It was with Samson that we began to see *why* Israel kept pursuing such a destructive course. In 14:3, Samson states why he wants to marry a woman that he knows God forbids. His reason, literally, is that, "she is right in my eyes" (and again in 14:7). This thing that is evil in God's eyes is right in Samson's.

The final two episodes in chapters 17–18 and 19–21 explore this theme further. In these accounts there are no judges. Instead, both stories revolve around the activities of two Levites, one who moves from Bethlehem in Judea to Ephraim, and another whose journey is in the opposite direction. This parallel suggests that both stories are to be read together with one big message.

In these chapters the phrase "Israel did evil in the eyes of the LORD" is not found. Instead, we hear a different refrain, literally: "In those days Israel had no king; everyone did what was right in his own eyes" (17:6 and 21:25). This alerts us to the change of perspective. Up until Samson, we were shown everything from God's point of view: we saw Israel's actions as evil in God's eyes, and our attention was directed to God's response of judgement and mercy. The final two stories show us what things looked like from *Israel's* perspective: not evil, but right in everyone's own eyes. These stories help us get under Israel's skin, to see why they were so set upon doing what was evil in God's sight.

Our last study showed us why idolatry was so attractive, and why it seemed so right in Israel's eyes. The final three chapters show us the other side of the coin. They show us how Israel still managed to do her own thing even when she kept all the correct externals in place. And it begins with one of the worst incidents recorded in the Bible...

Investigate

Read Judges 19:1-30

1. How would you describe the father-in-law's hospitality (19:3-10)?

2. What is ironic about the Levite's decision in 19:12?

3. *Read Genesis 19:1-13.* What parallels do you see with what happens at Gibeah?

4. What is your opinion of the Levite by the end? Why?

The events that occur in Gibeah are shocking. They are frighteningly similar to perhaps the most notoriously evil city in the Old Testament—Sodom. Only this time the culprits are part of the people of God. Things have gone radically wrong in Israel.

Even the Israelite institution of hospitality is infected by the prevailing evil. First, there is the over the top hospitality of the Levite's father-in-law that drags on and on. Then there is the refusal of anyone in Gibeah to take the Levite's party in. Finally, a person not from the city takes them in—and proves to be a model host. So much so, that he is prepared to sacrifice the women for his male guest. The events show that Israel's perception of right and wrong is so twisted that even something as straightforward as hospitality has been twisted.

But perhaps the most disturbing element in the story is the Levite himself. He sends his concubine out to the men to save his own skin. Then, judging by verse 27, the Levite goes to bed, unconcerned for her welfare. He only finds her in the morning because she is directly in his path to leave. His words to her seem callous and cold, "Get up, let's go". There is no suggestion that he has showed even the slightest concern for her appalling suffering. Finally, his actions in verse 29 are as extreme as they are attention provoking. How will Israel respond to this?

Investigate

Read Judges 20:1-48

1. On the chart below list the differences between the original account of the events in Gibeah, and the Levite's retelling of them:

Original account (19:22–29)	The Levite's version (20:4–6)

2. What does Israel decide to do? What is Benjamin's response? What is the result? (20:9-17)

3. Briefly summarize the events of Judges 20:18-45. Why do you think Israel was defeated the first two times if the LORD was directing them?

4. What is the outcome of the battle (20:46-48)? How do you feel about this?

If chapter 19 was shocking, then the events of chapter 20 show how far Israel has fallen. The book began with Israel enquiring of the LORD, "Who will be the first to go up and fight for us against the Canaanites?" And the LORD answers, "Judah". Now, at the end of her downward spiral of rebellion and disobedience, Israel is again enquiring of the LORD who shall go up first into battle, but this time it is against one of her own tribes. The LORD again answers that the first to go up will be Judah. The story has come full circle and Israel must wear the consequences of her constant rejection of the LORD.

Israel has gathered in response to the Levite's gruesome call. In fact, the Levite produces a greater assembling of Israel than that of any Spirit-endowed judge. The tribes hear the evidence, recognise the seriousness of the evil, and take steps to eradicate it. Benjamin assembles in support of Gibeah. The seriousness of the evil and the even greater evil of Benjamin in supporting the evil-doers is clear.

However, in the reporting of this great evil, the Levite is not telling the whole truth. He re-tells the events to his own advantage, maximising the threat to himself ("they were going to kill me") and neglecting to mention that he had sent out his concubine to satisfy the men's lust. His duplicity suggests that the tribal gathering is not completely reliable. While the tribes correctly saw the evil of Gibeah, they overlooked the character of the Levite. While they have done right this time, there is no guarantee they will get it right next time. The tribal assembly is no solution to the problem of everyone doing what is right in their own eyes.

Notwithstanding the Levite's role, the presence of an Israelite Sodom is a very serious matter. Israel's responsibility to purge the evil from within Israel is clear—as their words in verses 8-13 demonstrate.

But Benjamin then defeats Israel not once, but twice. Even worse is the fact that the LORD had been involved on Israel's side. What is going on?

It appears that the LORD is using Israel's battle with Benjamin as the means to punish all Israel. Israel's presumption before God, that we have seen right throughout Judges, is evident again as they speak with God. In verse 18, their only question is procedure—who will go first? After their defeat, they weep before God, in verse 23. This time they ask whether they should actually do battle and acknowledge that the Benjaminites are their kin. It is not until the second defeat that the Israelites fast and sacrifice to God (20:26). Now, for the first time, the whole decision is placed in God's hands—to abandon the battle as much as to pursue it. Before this, Israel had been merely keeping to the correct forms. Though they were seemingly seeking God's will, in truth they had merely been keeping up appearances. They looked to God to rubber stamp their decision. In return, God used the war of judgement on Benjamin to also judge Israel. Benjamin was judged for supporting Gibeah's evil, Israel for presuming upon God and taking his support for granted.

Third time round Israel is victorious. Unlike their conquest in chapter 1 that seems to have been abandoned as soon as they struck problems, they persist with their war on Benjamin despite two defeats. Israel shows more commitment to fighting their brothers than they ever did to fighting the Canaanites. In persistence they find victory—if only they had done this in the first place to the Canaanites!

They treat their fellow Israelites, the Benjamites, in precisely the way that they have not treated the Canaanites—with total destruction. When they are finished, only 600 soldiers are left out of the whole tribe. It looks as though one tribe will be lost from the people of God forever.

Investigate

Read Judges 21:1-25

1. What is the problem facing Israel?

2. What is Israel's first attempt to solve it?

3. How do they then try to solve it (21:5-14)? How legitimate is this do you think?

4. Summarise the third attempt (21:15-24). What is your opinion of this?

5. Evaluate Israel as you have seen them in Judges. What are they like?

6. What is the narrator's conclusion about the problem with Israel? (21:25)

This tragic episode began with the death of one woman at the hands of evil men. The events of Chapter 21 are made necessary by the death of all the women of a whole tribe at the hands of all Israel at the end of Chapter 20.

The story unfolds in two parts. Having made an unwise vow before the battle (like Jephthah) to not give their women to Benjamin, the Israelites now find themselves trapped. Their first solution is to engage in selective obedience. Finding one place that did not support the effort to cleanse the evil from Israel they enact their vow only part-way—a course that went against God's command that vows must be kept. They leave alive the eligible women and give them as wives. Still short, they hit upon a means whereby the Benjaminites can capture their wives in a raid. The raid had the blessing of the elders, but allowed them to avoid breaking the letter of their vow. Just like the hospitality in chapter 19, it is a farce of correctness. The proper procedures are all carried out with great dedication, but with the clear purpose of subverting the intention behind their vow. Their attitude to their own vows mirrors their attitude to God's covenant. They pay great attention to the details, but only so that they can wriggle out from the spirit of the Law. Pretending to obey, Israel circumvents God's rule.

The previous study revealed the attraction of false religion. These three chapters show the failure of Israel's religion even when it appeared true. All that we have read, happened in association with the house of the LORD served by genuine priests. The Levite was on his way to the house of the LORD when he stopped at Gibeah (19:18). Unlike the Danites, with their idolatrous shrine and ineligible priest, Israel approached God at the true shrine ministered by the true priest (20:27-28). They went through the right motions and used the correct procedures. Nonetheless, God did not approve of them. They inquired of God regarding the battle, and he used the battle to punish them. They inquired of God regarding the fate of Benjamin, and he remained silent. His punishment was to leave them in the situation they had made for themselves. Behind Israel's piety lay the belief that they could manipulate God by going through the right motions. They sought to use God's own religious system to control God. By his actions, God demonstrated that he is free to save and to judge.

By the end of Judges, one wonders what hope there is for Israel. This people is incurably idolatrous, and given over to doing what is right to them and wrong to God. None of the institutions in their society—customs of hospitality, the influence of the elders, the assembly of the whole nation, or even the true religion of God, has been able to restrain their disobedience. Despite God's continual judgement, and his continual grace by delivering them through the judges, Israel has only gotten worse. Israel shows us the plight of the human race: we are helplessly trapped by our own bias towards evil. We cannot stop doing what is wrong in God's eyes.

Yet this is not the only note on which Judges ends. There is also a note of hope, of new growth after the bushfires of Israel's sin. Despite the questionable methods used by Israel, the eventual outcome *is* positive. The breach within Israel is healed, the tribe of Benjamin continues. Verse 24 reminds us of the ending of the Abimelech saga: crisis over, life settles down again and everyone returns to normality. In fact, verse 24 is even more positive than its counterpart in 9:55, for in 21:24 we are reminded by the word 'inheritance' that behind all that we have witnessed in the book of Judges stands God's promises to bless and to save. Even the worst excesses of Israel's sin have not been able to overturn God's commitment to fulfil his promises.

Jesus the True King

The final verse, 21:25, points to how God would fulfil his promises despite the problem of our sin. Everyone did what was right in their eyes because they had no king. What we need is a ruler whose rule will overcome our sin.

In time, Israel obtained kings. This did not solve the problem of their sin. They no longer did their own thing but followed the lead of their ruler. However, Israel's kings proved to be just as disobedient as Israel had been. They led Israel away from God to idols and immorality. It became clear that, before God's promises could be fulfilled, a different king was needed—a king who would obey God. This ruler would deal with the problem of the sin of God's people.

Luke 23 recounts for us the great work of this king. In obedience to his Father, Jesus suffered crucifixion for us. Above his head was the written notice, "This is the King of the Jews" (Lk 23:38). He was proclaimed the true king of Israel in his death. And it is by his death for us that he removed the obstacle of our sin and cleared the way so that God's promises to bless would be fulfilled. Thus it was that Jesus could promise the dying criminal that he would be with Jesus in paradise that very day (Lk 23:42-43). Jesus' words were the proof that he was the true king and that his death was the solution to the sin of God's people. Through his death, Jesus opened the way for every person who turned from doing what was right in their own eyes and submitted to Jesus' rule to inherit God's promised blessing. It is the cross of Christ that is the solution to the problem that the book of Judges reveals. God's promises are fulfilled in Jesus. It is the great news of the gospel.

Think it through

1. How has Judges changed your understanding of God?

2. Reflect upon the different judges, and upon what you have seen of Israel in the last two studies. Where is the greatest temptation you face to act like Israel did? What steps can you take to prevent this?

3. How should the fact that Jesus' death dealt with the problem of your sin and enabled you to receive God's promised blessing affect your attitude to:

   • God?

   • Jesus?

   • yourself?

Who are we?

Ever since we opened our doors in 1991 as St Matthias Press, our aim has been to provide the Christian community with products of a uniformly high standard—both in their biblical faithfulness and in the quality of the writing and production.

Now known as The Good Book Company, we have grown to become an international provider of user-friendly resources, with Christians of all sorts using our Bible studies, books, Briefings, audio cassettes, videos, training courses and daily Bible reading resources.

Buy direct or from your local bookshop

You can order your resources either direct from us, or from your local Christian bookshop. There are advantages in both, but if you buy from us, you get these extra benefits:

- you save time—we usually despatch our orders within 24 hours of receiving them
- you save money—we have built-in discounts for bulk buying.
- you help keep us afloat—because we get more from each sale, buying from us direct helps us to invest more time and energy in providing you with the very best.

Please call us for a free catalogue of all our resources, including an up-to-date list of other titles in this Interactive Bible Studies series. Some details of IBS titles are contained on the following page.

Interactive and Topical Bible Studies

Our Interactive Bible Studies (IBS) and Topical Bible Studies (TBS) are a valuable resource to help you keep feeding from God's Word. The IBS series works through passages and books of the Bible; the TBS series pulls together the Bible's teaching on topics, such as money or prayer. As at June 2001, the series contains the following titles:

OLD TESTAMENT

FULL OF PROMISE
(THE BIG PICTURE OF THE O.T.)
Authors: Phil Campbell
& Bryson Smith, 8 studies

BEYOND EDEN
(GENESIS 1-11)
Authors: Phillip Jensen
and Tony Payne, 9 studies

THE ONE AND ONLY
(DEUTERONOMY)
Author: Bryson Smith,
8 studies

THE GOOD, THE BAD & THE UGLY (JUDGES)
Author: Mark Baddeley
10 studies

FAMINE & FORTUNE
(RUTH)
Authors: Barry Webb &
David Hohne, 4 studies

THE EYE OF THE STORM
(JOB)
Author: Bryson Smith,
6 studies

TWO CITIES
(ISAIAH)
Authors: Andrew Reid and
Karen Morris, 9 studies

KINGDOM OF DREAMS
(DANIEL)
Authors: Andrew Reid and
Karen Morris, 8 studies

BURNING DESIRE
(OBADIAH & MALACHI)
Authors: Phillip Jensen and
Richard Pulley, 6 studies

NEW TESTAMENT

THE GOOD LIVING GUIDE
(MATTHEW 5:1-12)
Authors: Phillip Jensen
and Tony Payne, 9 studies

NEWS OF THE HOUR
(MARK)
Author: Peter Bolt,
10 studies

FREE FOR ALL
(GALATIANS)
Authors: Phillip Jensen
& Kel Richards, 8 studies

WALK THIS WAY
(EPHESIANS)
Author: Bryson Smith,
8 studies

THE COMPLETE CHRISTIAN
(COLOSSIANS)
Authors: Phillip Jensen
and Tony Payne, 8 studies

ALL LIFE IS HERE
(1 TIMOTHY)
Authors: Phillip Jensen
and Greg Clarke, 9 studies

RUN THE RACE
(2 TIMOTHY)
Author: Bryson Smith,
6 studies

THE PATH TO GODLINESS
(TITUS)
Authors: Phillip Jensen
and Tony Payne, 6 studies

THE IMPLANTED WORD
(JAMES)
Authors: Phillip Jensen
and K.R. Birkett, 8 studies

HOMEWARD BOUND
(1 PETER)
Authors: Phillip Jensen and
Tony Payne, 10 studies

ALL YOU NEED TO KNOW
(2 PETER)
Author: Bryson Smith,
6 studies

TOPICAL BIBLE STUDIES

BOLD I APPROACH
(PRAYER)
Author: Tony Payne,
6 studies

CASH VALUES
(MONEY)
Author: Tony Payne,
5 studies

THE BLUEPRINT
(DOCTRINE)
Authors: Phillip Jensen
& Tony Payne, 11 studies

WOMAN OF GOD
Author: Terry Blowes
8 studies

THE MAN WHO MAKES A DIFFERENCE (EPHESIANS)
Author: Tony Payne
7 studies
This set of studies from Ephesians, is designed especially for men, and is sold as a separate leaders' guide and study guide

For an up-to date list visit:
www.thegoodbook.co.uk
or call 020-8942-0880